Two Worlds Apart Become One:
Pursuing the Christian Life 9,000 Miles Away

This book is dedicated to my wonderful husband Brent (Braxton) who is supportive of everything I decide to get involved in and is my biggest cheerleader. My son Harrison (Harry) who makes me laugh, and designed the front and back cover of my book. Also, to the many people who I have crossed paths within Australia and the United States. I am forever grateful to Tania Purser, who was the one that invited me to Heathmont Baptist Church where my life was forever changed.

Thank you to my American "sisters" Lori and Cheryl for encouraging me to write this book.

Note to the reader: I write often using Australian English words and expressions, so the American equivalent is provided immediately afterward in parenthesis.

Fair dinkum!

Scripture quoted is from; *The Holy Bible:* The New International Version. The Zondervan Corporation, 1984.

Chapter One

It was a beautiful sunny spring day in November at work, in Ferntree Gully, Australia, and I had just arrived back from lunch break after a walk around the block with a couple of my work colleagues, when Kat was informing me and other employees how she communicates with family in Malta on a chat site called "Make New Friends". I just shrugged it off, but she persisted that I set up an account. So I decided to set up an account and "Jaimme" as my handle.

People from all walks of life and all corners of the world joined in this chat room. My first chat was with a very nice woman from England by the name of Lucy. We chatted about our respective cultures and workplace. I chatted briefly as the boss was needing me to take minutes at a staff meeting. Australian employees are entitled to morning and afternoon tea breaks, so during my breaks I decided to join the chatroom once again. I was intrigued by "Braxton", an American, who engaged me with questions about my country, education, and hobbies. He informed me that he lived in Indiana, and was a school teacher at a public school high school, and that he taught Year 11 and 12 students (Grades 11 and 12). I was excited to chat with someone that had similar interests and was blown away by how this Internet "stuff" worked. I described to Braxton my job requirements which included organizing Professional Development programs for teachers, arranging interviews of principals and staff for placement in secondary schools, creating a database for all our students, and working closely with our speech pathologists, psychologist, and our curriculum advisers, as well as being secretary to the director.

I thought it rather ironic that not being a Catholic I was employed in the Catholic education system, but they couldn't discriminate as I had the relevant qualifications for the position offered. I would attend Catholic Mass, but I always thought that there was something missing in me. I could never quite put my finger on it. I was always searching for a deeper and richer understanding of what this "church" stuff was all about. I am so blessed by so many of my Catholic colleagues who became my friends, and who I love dearly.

Braxton had asked for my email address, and at that stage in my life I did not have a computer at home, I did not have a mobile phone with Internet, and I did not have an email account. Yes, Australia lagged behind the United States in computer technology at that time. After a couple weeks of thought and consideration, I decided to set up an email account and emailed Braxton. His response email was sent on Sunday 21 November. Braxton informed me that he was visiting his relatives in Michigan for Thanksgiving (something we don't celebrate in Australia), and how he was looking forward to being out of the classroom for a four day weekend. He had a very hectic school life, was involved in many after-school activities, was a member of his town's library board, and was an officer on his county's Republican Party Central Committee.

As time went on, the 16 hour time difference between the states of Victoria and Indiana was making it harder to connect via "Make New Friends", so most of our correspondence was done through lengthy emails. (In Indiana when it was 8:00 p.m. on a Thursday night it was 12:00 noon on a Friday in Victoria.) Braxton shared how Americans had a stronger church life and spiritual focus than much of the world, but like the world, these matters seemed to be the concern of fewer and fewer in society. I informed him that I was not "religious", but that in my younger years would attend the Anglican Church in my hometown of Olinda.

We continued to email back and forth, over the next few months, and during this time we became good friends. Braxton was focused on education and career and he had never met "Miss Right"…yet. He was an idealist and dreamer who was very romantic and had big dreams. A world apart, our words were powerful and eventually lead to a deeper sharing and especially about matters of faith. He shared the only way that life can be given real purpose is to come to a saving knowledge of Jesus Christ and to become Christ-like through the operation of the Holy Spirit; that he was born a sinner and came to see that Jesus was who He said He was; that in Him is redemption and Eternal Life, and that to have a personal relationship with Christ is the only way for any individual to find peace and contentment within themselves. True conversion causes the person to be changed in the heart because there is a removal of guilt for sins committed. He recommended that I read a book by C.S. Lewis called *Mere Christianity*, and to read my Bible on a daily basis. I was totally lost and confused by all of this "religion" stuff at first, but this caused me to ask many questions: What does it mean to have a relationship with Christ? What does one need to do? I prayed for my family every night, and I attended church once in a while. Isn't that enough? What does a Christian look like? What does salvation feel like?

Braxton found all my questions refreshing, and loved my honesty, and never found me to be a lesser person because my faith experience was totally different to his.

This is the same time that I started to be influenced as well by one of the speech pathologists, Tan Purser. Tan invited me to attend her Baptist Church, in which her husband was the Youth Pastor. I was excited at this prospect and looked forward to meeting her there. I arrived early and remember sitting in the carpark (parking lot) not really wanting to go in, as I felt a little sick to my stomach, and nervous, and thought to myself, "why am I here?", "why am I feeling this way?" A case of cold feet. People started arriving, and one couple pulled up next to me, so I felt awkward sitting in my car. I walked in with this couple, who of course realized that I was the new "kid" on the block. I walked up to the usher, received my bulletin, and felt as though my heart was about to jump out of my chest. Of course I was going to sit down in the back pew and hide so I didn't stand out, but a lovely older woman by the name of Dorothy Holdman who saw me waved me over to sit next to her. Dorothy made such an impact on my life. She was truly my mentor. She would phone me at least two to three times a week and pray with me. She would ask me how I was doing with my readings, and if I understood them.

After moving to the U.S., we started corresponding by written airmail letters to each other, and in one letter she told me she had the biggest fight in her life to face, and that she was dealing with colon cancer. This broke my heart, but she was at peace as she knew there was a much better place, and that she would be reunited with some of her family and friends in Heaven. I still carry one of her letters in my Bible to church every Sunday. Thank you, Dorothy, you truly touched my life, as well as many around you. You will never be forgotten. I love you.

Dr. John Smith, the senior pastor, preached about having a relationship with Jesus. Now the pastor was sounding more and more like Braxton. I was getting "hit" from both sides of the world. I was sure this service was directly pointed at me. At that very moment, I realized I needed to change my life and repent of the sins that had always hindered my life. On this day, May 14, I was saved. I was grateful that through the months of emails with Braxton, and the questions he had answered that I was set free from the bondage I had been in. Little did I realize in corresponding with Braxton, that he had planted the seed, and eventually would see my faith come to fruition. I could hardly contain my joy and excitement so headed straight to my workplace from church to send an email to Braxton, realizing that it was early hours in the morning over in the United States. It would be a few hours before I would get a reply. This was no easy feat to send this email because I had to phone security before I could enter the workplace, enter the code, and turn off the alarm, and hopefully be able to get logged onto to the Internet.

Chapter Two

Monday morning could not come soon enough as I wanted to share with Tan how the Holy Spirit had worked yesterday at church. I suggested to her that I would like to do a Bible Study at work during my lunchtime, and asked if she would be willing to help me grow in my spiritual walk. I choose the book of Romans. I am sure most new Christians would start with one of the Gospels, but no, not me, straight into a book that I knew nothing about and the book that was the most theological. We proceeded to meet every lunchtime. I had a real hunger to learn more, which led me to read my Bible every night, plus doing devotions in my quiet time. I had also started to play my Christian music in my office, and would also read *Our Daily Bread* (ironically a work that was produced just a few hours north of Braxton's home in Grand Rapids, Michigan) devotions aloud to some of my work colleagues each day. This was somewhat daunting to my Catholic colleagues, but they were very intrigued by the study I was doing, and the music I was now listening to, and asked many questions.

In the years preceding joining this chat room, my life had been in turmoil. I was divorced, my mother, who was my best friend had died at the age of 65 just one week after we had celebrated my 40th birthday, and I did not have a good relationship with my father.

My mother was a saintly woman who would give the shirt off her back. My father had many affairs behind my mother's back, and was very abusive to her, and honestly hated her. I would lay in bed waiting for my alcoholic father to arrive home from the closing hour at the pub. I would hear the car pull into the driveway, then the back door would slam. I would lay there my heart thumping that hard I thought it was going to come out of my chest, and tears would well up in my eyes. I would start praying, "Please God, don't let any of us be hurt tonight." This was my prayer every single night. Being the eldest was tough. I always felt as though I was the caretaker of our family. My mum would always have my dad's tea (supper as you call it in the States) sitting on a saucepan on the stove simmering away to keep it warm for when he arrived home. My dad would go into the bedroom where my mother was sleeping and would grab her by the hair and pull her out of bed. I would stand up to my father and verbally yell and scream at him to stop. On a few occasions, he would push me back against the wall. Ironically, he would sit stooped over his meal at the kitchen table, and would often break out in the hymn "Onward Christian Soldiers." To this day every time I hear this song being played, it takes me directly back to my childhood. My dad came from a Methodist background, so I wondered if this is a song he sang in his younger years. Why on earth he sang this song I have no idea. I have asked him this question, but he has never really given a precise answer. He would also kick us out of the house at all hours, and we would walk three houses up to our neighbors who would take us in for the night.

Putting up with this environment for 30 plus years was difficult. My mum was a forelady in a factory working to try and make ends meet, at the same time my father was blowing his money on alcohol. I was angry, bitter, and hurt. My mum struggled but always made sure we had food on the table each night, and clothes on our back. I also remember that most of my sister's and my clothes were all handmade by my lovely grandmother. I admired my grandmother and loved her so much. I was the first grandchild, and I had such a special bond with her. My maternal grandmother and grandfather actually lived with us for a short time, and this still did not stop my father's abusive behavior. He treated them just the way he treated us. They were heartbroken.

Whenever we went shopping with mum, which was usually on mum's payday, we shopped at a store called "Arndale" which was a 20 minute drive away. Myself, and my siblings would get so excited as this meant that we were getting brand new clothes, even though we had to wait for them. Mum would layby (layaway) our clothes and pay them off over a period of a couple of months. That two months seemed like years to us. I also remember stuffing my shoes with newspaper, as the soles had holes in them. After wearing them for a few hours the paper would disintegrate, and all would be left was your sock with a hole worn through it.

I would always cringe when my girlfriends wanted to come and hangout after school at my place, as I never knew what my father's attitude was going to be like and always found an excuse, and was happy to ride my bike to their place and play. As I got into my late teens, my house became a haven for all the young ones. The local girls and guys would hang out at my place. The "locals" thought it was a cool thing to do, and looking back we had so much fun. My mum at Christmas time would make sure that if anyone was by themselves they were to come and spend Christmas Day with us. This was also something that my father actually supported.

Mum would prefer for us to bring our friends home, and most Saturdays before we went to follow our local football team Olinda, she would have a great big pot of pea soup on the stove, or toasted sanga's (sandwiches).

Chapter Three

I felt greatly for my brother, for as much as he tried to have a relationship with my dad, he could never do anything right no matter how much he tried. He would be out trying to help dad in the garage, and my father would swear at him, and call him useless, and put him down. My mum was always playing the role of both mum and dad.

The surprising thing is that we never really went without, as my aunties knew the situation my mum was in and helped out with gifts at Christmas, birthdays, and special occasions. Mum would always tell us that dad loved us, and was very proud of the three of us, but he would never share this with any of us. It was mum that held us together and was the backbone of our family. I remember walking to the bus stop in my high school years, exhausted, hurt, feeling not worthy of anything, not being able to talk about it, and smiling to friends and teachers as if everything was just fine and dandy, when in actual fact I was becoming withdrawn, and probably suffering from depression, but back then depression was not really talked about.

My father was the local constable (policeman) in the township of Olinda and was well respected and liked. Little did most townspeople know that my dad was like Dr. Jekyll and Mr. Hyde. My dad eventually did slow down his drinking habit, but he was still a bitter man. When my mother died suddenly from a pontine hemorrhage I then knew she was free at last and would never have to face this torment ever again, and that one day we would be reunited in Heaven. I knew deeply that this was God's plan for her. It was difficult to understand as to why she would want to stay with my father under these circumstances, and her response was always the same: "I stay with him because of you three children". My Mother was an amazing woman. Always volunteering or helping out at various events, making biscuits (cookies) or scones for people, and always putting others first before herself. She was well loved in her community and left a great legacy. My prayer is to do you proud mum.

I do not have any regrets whatsoever about my upbringing, as this made me the person I am today. From a family that was very dysfunctional, we three kids could have easily gone off the rails. And at times in my life, I did. I wasn't the perfect angel by any means. I was the one out partying and never obeying the curfew set by my mother. I became very rebellious.

As soon as my siblings and myself earned an income, and were still living at home, we would pay board (rent) to mum. We would all pay $30 a week. This would contribute to help pay the bills. In my high school years I would get off the bus around 3:30 p.m. and walk over to the factory where mum worked and would do a few hours work for extra money.

As I write this I have to chuckle as my mum was so proud of the three of us, and would always "brag" about our positions we held in the workplace and was quick to tell anyone about us. It was somewhat embarrassing, but it was truly okay. I just loved my mum. I wish that everyone could have known my mum.

Not long after my mum's death, I thought it was time to write a handwritten letter to my dad outlining what I did not like about him, what he had done to our family, and how disappointed I was in him for committing adultery, but at the same time I was also asking for forgiveness. A week after my mum had passed he was already with someone else. Talk about a knife piercing through my chest. He received my letter, and never responded, so I prayed about it, and built up the courage to finally phone him. To have any further contact with my father, and to finally have some sort of peace, I knew it was time to forgive him. Easy? – Heck no! We talked, and then I said, "I need to forgive you for all the things that have happened in the past, the way we were treated, what you did to mum, and how you made our life Hell". He was quiet with me over the phone, but I am grateful that he never hung up on me.

Chapter Four

As time passed my dad was having health issues, and in May 2011 he underwent surgery to have a heart valve replacement done. His specialist informed me that it was a risky surgery and at age 80 was not sure whether he would survive it. My sister and I would take it in turns of visiting him in hospital; she would do the morning shift and I would do the afternoon shift. The afternoon before surgery I had asked him if he had a personal relationship with Jesus. I continued to explain what he needed to do, and what that entailed. He listened intently. When I asked again if he understood what I just had explained at first I got a weird and concerned look, but he replied, "Don't worry Shelley. I know where I am going, and I will see you on the other side." I knew then that I would see him again, which gave me a sense of peace and comfort.

I am getting ahead of my story here, but my father and I have had the best relationship in the last 19 years that we have ever had. All praise and glory to God! We would contact each other three to four times a week, and we would visit from America every couple of years and stay with him. He loves my husband Braxton, myself, and grandson Harrison. Dad often calls Harrison "Oscar" as that is what he has called his other grandsons. He took an interest in Harrison and what he was involved in at school and would look forward to us visiting. He always, to this day, asks after all of us. Unfortunately, he has been in ill health for the last few years and has been hospitalized for the last three months with continuing congestive heart failure, diabetes complications, and kidney failure. It has been quite the ordeal, and I am thankful that my sister and brother-in-law have been there for him at all times. Kerryn has done such a wonderful job as caretaker, and I love how compassionately she dresses his open ulcers on his legs, helps him getting dressed, drives him to his doctor's appointments, does his laundry, makes his bed, cleans his house, cuts his hair, and not once have I ever heard her complain about doing these things. She is not only running dad's household, but also her own, and she also works three days a week on top of all of this. My brother-in-law Boofie has been instrumental too in taking dad to some of his doctor's appointments, visiting him in hospital, and really being a support for Kerryn.

My niece Mickie and nephews Bretto and Lukey have helped with some of these things as well. Most importantly, they sit with dad and watch Aussie Rules footy (football) on a Friday evening, and just spend valuable time with him one-on-one, and this has given Kerryn a deserved break. Dad loves all his grandkids very much. On my visits to dad in October and again in December 2017, I was glad to help out, and relieve Kerryn, so that she could have one-on-one time with Boofie. I enjoyed spending time with dad, knowing that these days were so precious. My brother Rob, his wife Julie ("Harry"), and my nephews Scotty and Dan live in Perth, but have been instrumental in phoning him, and making the four hour flight from Perth to Melbourne when possible.

Positive memories of my dad are connected to his role as police officer and a fisher. On January 16, 1965 while a constable stationed at Olinda he rescued 120 Jewish teenagers, who were attending a youth conference at the Georgian Guest House in Olinda when a fire broke out in the boiler room. For his brave action, he was awarded the Royal Humane Society Award of Merit certificate and medal by her majesty H.R.H. Queen Elizabeth II.

On October 23, 1969 (my father's birthday) my dad and his senior sergeant "Wicks" were called to an altercation at the local "Cuckoo Restaurant" in our hometown. This resulted in "Wicks" receiving a fractured skull and my father with severe facial lacerations. My Mum would not let us into his bedroom because it would have been too distressing to see his injuries. My father is a very brave man indeed.

During my younger years, I would always go out fishing with my dad, and sometimes my other siblings would come along as well. I was dad's "fisher girl" as he sometimes called me. I would get up at 5:00 a.m. on a weekend, and dad and I would head down to Rosebud where we had a fishing boat which we had named "Diane" moored on Port Philip Bay. The drive would take an hour, and I would sit next to him on the bench seat in our station wagon, and lean on his shoulder and sleep until we arrived. I would wade out in the murky water, with seaweed slapping around my legs, the sharp shells piercing the bottom of my bare feet, and the water sometimes up to my neck. I would unmoor our boat, and bring it up to the jetty where dad was waiting for me with our bait and fishing gear.

Dad had all the fishing spots marked out. We would spend hours and hours out on the bay. We never used fishing rods out on our boat, instead dad would cut two "V" shapes out of each end of a piece of plywood and would wind fishing line around it, and then attach our homemade sinkers, and hook. As "Diane" was also used as a chartered fishing boat, using this method took up less room than everyone having a fishing rod. I would love how "Diane" would move up and down, and side to side as she was cutting through the waves, and everything seemed so perfect and serene. We would get so far out on the bay that you could no longer look back to see the foreshore. Every which way you looked we were surrounded by water and in the very distance we could still make out Arthur's Seat which is a lookout over Port Phillip Bay. Once moored we would bait our lines, drop them over the side and wait for fish to bite. The fun part was you never knew what sort of fish you were going to bring up. Flathead was my favorite fish to catch and eat. Like our poisonous snakes, and spiders, we also have poisonous fish. Dad had taught me which ones to watch out for. I also caught quite a lot of seaweed in my fishing days which would have muscles, cockles, and oysters attached to it. He would use a sharp knife, apply pressure and oscillate around the hinge to open them. We would then eat them raw. Quite often you would see the dolphins frolicking, and it was not uncommon to see sharks swimming around the boat.

Never really thought much about it then, but I am sure I would feel differently about it now.

My father has a great sense of humor, and we are thankful that his mind is still as sharp as a tack, but his body is becoming like withered leaves that have fallen before winter sets in. I know his days are numbered on this earth, but rejoice that we will see each other again. I am not saying this is an easy ride to endure, but it is the inevitable. My dad is awesome, and I tell him with every phone call that I love him, and that I am praying for him. After all these years I no longer envy other daughter-father relationships, because I have one. Praise God for this! I know that when the time comes for my dad to leave this earth I will be reunited with both my parents one day and what a day that will be!

I listened to Pastor Jim bring the message at my church on how the "quality and quantity of your life is impacted by your relationship with your parents." I honor and respect my father. Friends do not carry this burden of not having a relationship with your parents, as hard as it may be, it also sets you free, and brings peace to your soul. "Children, obey your parents in the Lord, for this is right. Honor your father and mother"—which is the first commandment with a promise—"so that it may go well with you and that you may enjoy long life on the earth." (Ephesians 6: 1-3)

It was such a blessing that my son Harrison, and I got to visit Christmas 2017, and for the first time in 17 years my siblings, my niece, and nephews were together. To think back to this day chokes me with tears as it was such a special time for all of us. I have my good and bad days, as I have no other family members living in the States, and my husband is an only child, so we only have a couple of Braxton's cousins that we keep in contact with. I am grateful beyond measure that Harrison got to spend valuable time with Poppa. I would not have got through any of this without prayer. I had my pastor's wife, two of my closest friends, my small group, women's ministry Core Team, my American mama, and my accountability partner praying for me daily.

Chapter Five

From my family past and present, I now return to my developing relationship with Braxton. He started to nickname me "Joey" in his emails, which he still calls me today. (A "joey" is a baby kangaroo.)

Braxton and I would continue to write emails weekly, and I would continue to ask questions I had in relation to the Bible and Christianity. His emails were lengthy and scripture based. A couple of the questions I asked were:

Why does God keep some things from us?
"The secret things belong to the LORD our God, but the things revealed belong to us and to our children forever, that we may follow all the words of this law." (Deut. 29:29)

Explain what it means to have the mind of Christ?
"Who has known the mind of the Lord so as to instruct Him?" (1 Cor. 2:16)

He was always so encouraging and always wanted me to seek to know the things of God with all of my heart. I knew that God was faithful to help me along the way and that He only asks that I am to be genuine and desirous of knowing Him and His truth.

After communicating for several months we both knew that our friendship was taking the form of a relationship, and that we had fallen madly in love with each other, and that there had been a flame ignited between us. We really got to know each other through our emails. Yet, how in the world was a long distance relationship ever to work when we were worlds apart? Leaving one's country, leaving family, the costly immigration process, marriage, and different cultures: Who was going to give up what? These questions we talked at length about and earnestly prayed about.

I decided to make the trek to the United States to meet his mum (mom) and him in person in July 2000. This would also be the time we exchanged photos, which made sense as I needed to know who to look for when I arrived. My going to meet with this "guy" caused much distress for my dad and siblings. Meeting a stranger in a foreign land sounds crazy and meeting Online still causes many to cringe. I just need to stop here and say that I am such the adventurous type, and having traveled to other countries was not a big deal in my mind. I backpacked around New Zealand and visited Bali, Indonesia numerous times. I guess you could say that I always lived life on the "edge". I believe that because I was 40 and mature, that this did not pose a problem, nor seemed to be a huge deal to me. I had also had phone contact with Braxton's mother, and she knew that I was coming, and looking forward to meeting me.

I have to laugh now, but Braxton is so organized that he even had it down to the temperatures it would be in July when I would visit, what clothes I needed to bring….clothes for church, theater, a student's wedding, dining out, dress shoes, sandals, and runners… that is my complete wardrobe I thought. Then in his last line to me he said "travel light, your friendly travel consultant, Braxton Savchuk, Hoosier Holidays Inc." I still laugh at this today.

Chapter Six

My day to depart to the U.S. was July 3rd. I had booked my ticket with Japan Airlines and had a stopover in Tokyo. Let me tell you, those planes are tiny, and those Asian's know exactly how to get comfortable. Once seated and buckled into their seat, they place their slippers on, eye masks on, place their feet up on the seat and crouch into a ball, and off to sleep they go. All before I got my seatbelt fastened. First off I have thunder thighs and wide hips and my hips were pushing so hard against the armrests that I was bruised on my arrival into Japan. Food on the plane was not for the faint hearted. Raw fish and something I just could not make out, but looked somewhat like fish eyes floating around in this brown looking broth. The first time being in Tokyo, and only knowing one word in Japanese was "Kon'nichiwa" which means "hello", yet I felt pretty good being able to say hello to everyone, but was lost if anyone replied, because I have no idea what they were saying. I did find where I needed to go to get on the airport shuttle which would take me to this fancy hotel for my overnight stay. I checked in and proceeded to the lifts (elevator) to my room.

Tired from the trip, I decided to freshen up, get my pee jays on and the beautiful kimono and white toweling slippers that the hotel provided. After a late arrival, I was famished, so I was grateful after rummaging through my handbag to find a protein bar. I was also very parched and had noticed that there was a vending machine not too far from my room, so I proceeded down the hallway to purchase a Diet Coke. On my way back to my room I then realized that I did not have the key card to let me back in. Alas! That meant that dressed for bed, I had to go down to the busy reception area. The queue (line) at the reception area was practically out the door as I waltzed up to the counter with hundreds of Asian eyes directed at me wondering what this strange western woman was doing. I threw my arms up in the air and said, "I know! I know! I locked myself out of my room", which caused the entire foyer to erupt into great laughter.

The next morning, I boarded the airport shuttle and headed back to the airport to resume my flight to O'Hare Airport at Chicago. I was weary, anxious, excited, and nervous, but looked forward to finally meeting Braxton face to face.

I had purchased souvenirs from Australia for Rhea (Braxton's mum) which consisted of *Angela Ashes* by Frank McCourt, a tea mug featuring the national flower of Australia (the Golden Wattle), and for Braxton socks with the Australian flag on them, a jar of Vegemite (a staple in Australian homes that we spread on white bread or dry biscuits (crackers)). A ruler in centimeters (a standing joke between Braxton and myself is that he thinks everything measured should be done with the U.S. measurement), a tie with the Australian flag on it, lollies (candy), and (of course) a plush kangaroo.

Previous to my departing for the States, Braxton had already met with his pastor and his wife to give them the rundown on me, and how we had met Online. They were very keen to meet me. Braxton's mum likewise knew that he had communicated with me, and she really had no reservations about us, as we were both in our 40's and mature enough to be meeting. I think deep down that she did not think much would evolve from it, especially as I had siblings and all my family back home, and so she felt quite safe that I was not going to be taking her son away from her. She always had a vision that Braxton would marry a woman from his church, but God had different plans. Braxton had moved also back home during his father's illness to help his mum care for him.

Meeting face to face for the first time confirmed everything ever written or shared between us in our emails. He was handsome, sophisticated looking, funny, very intelligent and witty, and a true gentleman. I loved everything about him. I was easy to spot as we often joke about it now, but I was the only western woman on that plane as I walked through the doors with my fellow Asian travelers. But just in case, I had placed the stuffed kangaroo in the side pocket of my carry-on as a distinguishing marker. Looking into each other's eyes is a moment that neither of us will ever forget. After some initial words, we proceeded to the carpark (parking lot) loaded my luggage in the boot (trunk) and headed to Ligonier, Indiana where I would be staying with his mother Rhea and him in his family home.

Some first impressions on arriving here: I observed that everyone seems to know only one speed, and that is fast; that there are huge billboards lining the side of the highways; that driving on the wrong side (or right side) of road felt weird, and that the industrial side of Gary, Indiana is depressing. We talked and talked, and Braxton being such the history buff filled me in on the various towns that we drove through and their history. He even shared things about my country that I did not know. Braxton is ever the teacher.

Feeling weary and hungry Braxton pulled off at an exit to a Macca's (McDonald's). This was going to be quite the experience as I wanted to see how different it was to the Australian version. I was wanting to order a toastie (toasted sandwich) and a cappuccino, only to realize that both did not exist. I chose a Big Mac, but noticed how sweet the bun was. Braxton ordered chips (fries) and emptied them from the container onto his serviette (napkin) that he already had poured some tomato sauce (ketchup) on. I must have given a strange look, and said, "You eat chips with sauce? Ah no! "

We got back into the car and feeling quite satiated my eyelids were now starting to get heavy, and I was having a hard time trying to stay awake. Before too long I dozed off. I remember waking up just before we arrived in Ligonier. It was a sunny day, and I noticed how green the grass was, and the beautiful red tulips that had been strategically planted in unison along the footpath. Rhea came out and greeted me. The long journey left me looking frazzled and I certainly did not look like a movie star. First thing I did was ask to use the phone to let my family back home know that I had arrived safely at Braxton's mum's house. My family were greatly relieved.

Braxton made us all a cuppa (cup), with British tea bags; the best drink I had had since departing home. I then excused myself as I wanted to shower, unpack some of my goodies, and to change into clean clothes. Feeling somewhat human, I brought the souvenirs out to pass out to Rhea and Braxton. We chatted briefly before I started to wilt, so retired to bed early.

Laying on this soft comfortable bed and staring up at the fan that was making a whirring sound as it turned around, and drifting in and out of sleep, felt surreal. I was really here, and in the presence of this man with whom I had communicated with for the last 10 months. As I turned to lay on my side, I winched and groaned and soon remembered about my bruised hips. I pulled myself off the bed and got up to turn the light off, only to notice that the fan also went off. Confused, I thought how on earth do I keep the fan on? This was a new thing for me as we do not have ceiling fans that include lights in Australian homes. After pulling this chain and that chain, I managed to work it out. Off into a deep sleep I went ready to face the next day.

I awoke to the birds chirping, the sun trying to peek through the half-drawn curtains, realizing that it must be late morning. The house was quiet and I could not hear any stirring. I quietly walked out, and Braxton and Rhea were sitting and talking softly as they did not want to wake me. I was hungry and looking forward to a hearty breakfast, and hoping it was not going to be donuts and coffee. I had assumed that was all Americans ever ate. Australians drink tea and do not consume sweet foods for brekkie (breakfast). Braxton cooked up scrambled bumnuts (eggs), which were served with toast. One thing I did notice, however, was the sweetness of the bread, and the different taste in the butter. I smothered my toast in Vegemite, which made it bearable to eat.

Braxton tried Vegemite for the first time and found it a bit potent, but he had spread it on too thick. Luckily he was not repulsed by this yeast extract spread.

My three-week stay in the States consisted of meeting his pastor and his wife, attending 4th of July celebrations with Braxton's extended family at a cousin's lake property in Michigan, meeting church friends of Braxton, as well as attending a three-day church camp at Taylor University in Upland, Indiana. Truth be known I was a little anxious about this church camp and had no idea what to expect. I knew we would be attending one seminar on Friday night, a Saturday night service, and then a worship service on Sunday. The rest of the time I spent in a women's prayer group, where Michelle took me under her wing. It was a fun time of fellowship. I enjoyed listening to the speakers of the seminars and found the preaching services were deep and meaningful. The other memory I have of this camp is the great ice cream place just down the road called "Ivanhoe's". A popular local hangout for many of the students that attend Taylor University.

I enjoyed my many walks around Kenney Park which is located at the back of Braxton's mum's property, walked past the beautiful old Jewish homes that adorn the streets of Ligonier, visited the Jewish Museum, and always found a trip to Owen's Supermarket was intriguing to check out the different food items. Enjoyed meals at Braxton's friend's homes, a tour of his school and classroom, and a picnic at Pokagon State Park. It was a fun-filled packed three weeks.

My time in the States felt as though I was on "show", because people were so intrigued with the Australian accent, and always seemed to be taken back whenever I spoke. Whenever we were out at a restaurant, and as soon as I would speak, the waiter or waitress just stared at me. Firstly in shock because of the accent, and, secondly, having no idea of what I had just said. Quite often I was never understood, and Braxton would interpret for me. It was frustrating at times.

Chapter Seven

Australians hear the Yankee accent daily, because of all of the American television and movies that flood our culture, but Americans do not hear Aussies speak often. My three weeks left other observations about the U.S.: the weak coffee; the amount of food that is piled on your plate; iced coffee is just coffee and ice blocks (cubes); iced tea; there must be 100 different salad dressings; sweet donuts and bread; no morning or afternoon tea breaks in the workplace; short lunch breaks; only two weeks (not four) weeks annual leave (vacation) after commencing work for an employer; no 13 weeks paid long service leave after being with a company for 10 years; everyone is in a hurry; only six weeks (not 12 months) fully paid maternity leave; and no paid paternity leave of three months for the husband; you do not just knock on someone's door and spend the afternoon with them; and drive-up banks and chemists (drug stores) abound.

Moving to another westernized country is not really different, but is still a culture shock. Living abroad, however, not only broadens your horizon, but it makes you appreciate other cultures as well as your own. People are interesting. I truly appreciate and love the American people and culture even with all its differences.

What I was especially intrigued with was the Amish who populate Northeastern Indiana. I had never seen or heard about the Amish culture and found it interesting, to say the least. There are a couple of things that the Amish and Australians have in common: both hang their clothes out on a clothesline, and cook everything from scratch. The only time Australians ever visit a restaurant is really for special occasions, such as birthdays and family get-togethers.

I took two "faceless" handmade Amish dolls back with me, as well as an Amish cookbook. The Amish dress is very plain and conservative. They have no electrical power, use kerosene lamps for lighting, and I observed most houses were painted white. I loved their easy and free lifestyle that is less materialistic. The Amish actually understood my accent more so than the Americans. I also could not believe how flat Indiana is with a landscape of one cornfield after another cornfield, and after another cornfield. Where were the hills and valleys that I was used to? Indiana summer was quite different to mine, in that it was very hot and humid. Our summers are hot, but mostly a dry heat. Braxton then informed me about the winter here. Snow! That white stuff we have in our mountains if you want to go snow skiing. I was not having anything to do with that I told him.

Braxton took me to a quaint little place called the Honeyville General Store which is near Topeka, Indiana. This place had everything you wanted in relation to Amish souvenirs. What a fun place. We toured Shipshewana, Middlebury, and many other wonderful places that seemed to be off the beaten track—all in Amish country.

I remember eating at a little Amish-style restaurant called "Tiffany's" in Topeka where we had a traditional Amish meal consisting of chicken and noodles, homemade bread with Amish peanut butter (this is peanut butter mixed with marshmallow spread), and shoo-fly pie. Shoo-fly pie is a molasses pie baked in a pie crust. This pie was developed by the Pennsylvania Dutch back in the 1880's. I can truly say I am not a fan of Amish peanut butter as it is sickly sweet, and the pie is definitely a required taste. Again Australians tend not to consume sugar like the Americans do.

We were now starting to count the days we had left together, and knew they were approaching fast. Braxton and I knew that we were right for each other and that the only way this long distance relationship was to ever work would have to be a God thing. We prayed, and had others praying for us to make this crooked path straight if it was God's will. Packing to leave was a bitter-sweet moment for both of us.

Braxton drove me to Chicago, and unlike my trip from Chicago to Ligonier, it was somewhat subdued. Neither of us spoke much, but would glance over at each other and smile. We had arrived at O'Hare early in time to have a coffee and a quick bite to eat. Braxton purchased two muffins and our coffees whilst I found a table. We sat across from each other with tears welling up in both of our eyes, knowing that the next time we would see each other would be five months away. Believe me, this was torture. He prayed as we held hands, and tears ran down my cheeks, my mascara stinging my eyes, but believing that God was with us. We said our farewells as he walked me to the gate. I could not look back, as I was a blubbering wreck. I composed myself as I had to proceed through security (pre-9/11) and headed to the gate to catch my plane. Once I had boarded the plane and sat down I was reminded that I was going to have bruised hips again, but hoping it would not be as bad as my trip over as I was lucky enough to book an aisle seat.

This guy had a piece of my heart, and I knew then that I had fallen deeply in love with a Christian man who loved God. I know that because of God's love and mercy is what brought us together.

Feeling total exhausted after a very long flight, I arrived at Tullamarine Airport, Melbourne where my brother Rob was waiting to collect me and drive the 50-minute trip home. My brother had previously spoken with Braxton on the phone to make sure he was going to take care of his sister. I shared with him my trip, and more about Braxton and his mum, and what Indiana was like, and how he would get to meet Braxton in December. I phoned Braxton to let him know that I arrived safely home, and how great it was to hear his voice. We chatted briefly before I headed to bed. At work, the following day I could hardly focus and felt like a zombie. My boss let me go home early to catch up on my sleep. Thinking back I should have taken an extra day off. I struggled with jet lag for the entire week. From door to door one way my trip was a total of 55 hours.

Now the time had come to start counting down the days until Braxton would arrive in December 2000 to meet my family. This would be during his school break, but unfortunately, he could only stay for one week. Believe me, we had been separated for five months, so I would be happy just to see him for one day. Our summer months are December through to February, and temperatures can range in the 90-120F. I told him to pack light – shorts and tees.

When the day of his arrival came, I drove my MGBGT out to the airport to pick him up. I arrived early, and thankfully his plane was on time. Just for the record, this trip is long and exhausting. First time doing it is a novelty, but believe me that the novelty soon wears off. I saw him walk out from the customs door area and ran up to him, gave him the biggest hug and kiss and was giddy with excitement. Yes, even in your 40s you can still feel that way. The week that he was here happened to be one of the coldest weeks we had during our summer. With this being the case, he did need to purchase some warmer clothing. Unfortunately, his luggage never arrived with him, but it was delivered to my sister's house the following day. Fortunately, he had packed a change of clothes in his carry-on. I was ready and wanted to show my man my world.

After locating the car at the airport terminal, I laughed at Braxton as he had walked around to the driver's side to get in. I did the same thing when visiting him. Yes, it takes quite some time to get used to getting into opposites sides of the car when both countries are different, and driving on the opposite side of the road can feel daunting. After such a grueling flight I did not want him driving through heavy Melbourne traffic, but to be honest, I did not want him driving my MG which was a four on the floor.

Chapter Eight

My sister's place is approximately a 35 kilometers (22 miles) drive from Melbourne. Roads heading out of Melbourne up to Olinda are winding, and are not great if you suffered from any kind of motion sickness. It was fun for Braxton to experience my racing expertise through some of those corners in my MGBGT (I did my motor racing in this car).

On the ride he talked about his flight with United, as we drove back to my sister's place. I was looking forward to Braxton that evening meeting my brother and his family as well as my dad for the first time.

As we got out of the congestion and slow going traffic from Melbourne and headed towards the Dandenongs, he made the comment on the towering trees that adorned each side of the road as we progressed closer to "home". These trees are known as Mountain

Ash. The Mountain Ash is the world's tallest flowering tree and can reach heights of 150 meters (492 feet). Interesting to note here in the States, that the only other species that comes a close second in height is the Californian Redwood (Sequoia Sempervirens).

The Dandenong Ranges consist of mostly rolling hills, steep valleys, and gullies, and is heavily covered with tree ferns, and heavy undergrowth. In the early days, the Dandenong Ranges was used as a major source of timber for Melbourne. The Dandenong Ranges even going back to the 1870's was popular with day trippers. This is still the case today. Living here is like living in a rainforest. It can be damp, wet, and foggy in the winter months, and sometimes we may have snow, that does not really amount to anything, and the summers can be so hot and dry that we are often placed under a Total Fire Ban Risk, which means we are not allowed to burn off or have barbies (barbeque) due to the high risk of starting a bushfire. The population of my hometown Olinda is approximately 1500. Although it seems to be set in a rural area, the mountain makes up Melbourne's eastern suburban fringe.

Meeting family we had a very late evening, and I know we all looked forward to heading to bed for a good night's rest. When dad and Braxton had some alone time together, Braxton had asked for my hand in marriage. My dad had known my feelings for Braxton, just like the rest of my family had known. I knew with my leaving my country, and my home roots, that this was going to be tough on everyone when the day would finally come.

I was looking forward to "showing off" my hometown this time. Braxton was in awe at the size of the camellia bushes that were 8 to 10 feet tall and in full bloom, hydrangeas that spanned 10 feet in diameter with the different shades of blue, purple, and pink, and the blue and white flowers of the agapanthus that stood 8 feet tall by the side fence of my sister's and brother in laws property.

As I made my way downstairs to the kitchen, my sister had already commenced breakfast for all of us. It was like feeding time at the zoo. Breakfast consisted of toast and vegemite, a cup of Dilmah tea, muesli, and Nutri Grain cereal (a Kellogg's brand). No donuts! Braxton was the last one to arrive down for brekkie, as I wanted him to catch up on as much sleep as possible. My niece and nephews had been anxiously waiting for him to make an appearance.

I planned most of the day's activities and was hoping that I would not tire him out too much. First up was visit to St Matthew's Anglican Church on Monash Avenue where I attended as a child. My mum would take myself, and my siblings to church every Sunday, and Youth Group every Friday evening. Next stop was St. Michael's and All Angels' Anglican Church which was approximately 3.9 km (2.4 miles). It was one church, but had two different sites. I took my confirmation at this church the year of 1973 by the then Bishop R.W. Dann, Diocese of Melbourne.

On checking my watch I realized it was morning tea time. Time for a cuppa and homemade scones (not like the scones in the States) with jam and whipped cream (heavy cream whipped until stiff). This is what is known as Devonshire Tea. The scone, made with self-rising flour, is what in America is a biscuit and not a sweet triangular pastry. I drove to a little tea room where I used to work on weekends known as Churinga. "Churinga" is actually an aboriginal word meaning "an object carved from wood or stone" by an Aboriginal tribe. It was nice to revisit this place as I had not stepped foot in it for years. I ordered our pot of tea, and scones, while Braxton was distracted by the loud birds outside the window. Not like the little songbirds that he was used to in Indiana. The sulphur-crested cockatoo is a pretty looking bird with a bright yellow crest, but they have a very loud squawking sound, and will quite often wake you up of a morning. Between the cockatoo and our Magpie which is a medium-sized black and white bird which also has a distinct sound, I remember walking to school and the Magpie would come down and swoop your head as they became aggressive during breeding season. Thankfully it wasn't breeding season at the time of Braxton's visit.

We got back in the MG and headed down to Sassafras which is a short distance from the main township of Olinda. Parked the car and walked along both sides of the footpath (sidewalk), and visited the many wonderful shops. Miss Marple's is a cute little tea room, and next door we visited Tea Leaves where he purchased Australian loose tea to take back home for his mother, the unique but expensive clothing shops, the puppeteer shop, and walked up to where I once attended kindergarten. It was a walk down memory lane for me.

Leaving Sassafras we headed to Monbulk. Monbulk is where I attended high school – years 7-12. (High school is six years not four years in Australia.) We went into the local bakery and purchased two pasties, and a cold drink and headed to Grant's Picnic Ground in Kallista for our little picnic. Surrounded by cockatoos, which we got to feed, along with the Rosellas (which is a medium-sized bird vibrant in color). The coloring differs depending on the species, but they are either a vibrant red and blue color or green, blue and red color. Surrounded by the Mountain Ash trees, we felt like we were in paradise. As we sat and ate our pasties we talked about how wonderful it was to be in each other's company again.

We had a full day, and it was nice to eventually get home, put our feet up awhile before evening tea (supper) would be served. Our menu tonight was roast lamb, roasted vegetables, gravy and pavlova for dessert. In Australia, we plate every meal (not "family style"). I still do this today, and I prefer this, as you do not tend to overeat. It is also acceptable to not finish what is on your plate. We are not offended, and it is completely acceptable if you would like seconds. After our meal, we resided in the lounge room (family room) to watch telly (TV), and to tell the family about the places we visited. It was a fun and bonding time for Braxton to get to know his "new" family.

The following day we continued to do all the touristy things around my hometown. Walked some of the nature trails, walked up to the TV towers, and visited the local bakery where we had flat white coffees and lamingtons. Later that afternoon we drove down to Croydon and Dandenong to introduce Braxton to my relatives. One set of relatives were inquisitive about the States and asked many questions. My Auntie Lorna had once traveled to the States, so it wasn't anything new for her. Later that evening my brother had made reservations at Marybrooke Restaurant in Sherbrooke Forest, which was originally known as the Baron of Beef. Restaurants in my hometown are very popular for weddings of celebrities, and on weekends you could hardly move due to busloads of tourists coming up from Melbourne. My brother was friends with the owners of Marybrooke, so we were treated like royalty. We enjoyed a wonderful, romantic meal, and enjoyed our time together.

Chapter Nine

A trip to Downunder would be amiss if I didn't take Braxton to my workplace, to see where all this "chat" commenced from, and to have a visual of what my office looked like. My Office was located in part of the old convent. Braxton got to meet Kat who was the one that introduced me to the chat room. I also wanted him to meet my boss and other work colleagues who were also my friends. I introduced Braxton to Tan who was instrumental in my spiritual walk. My girlfriend Neats had arranged a morning tea for us, with all the Aussie trimmings.

We ventured out fairly early the next morning to Healesville Sanctuary, which is approximately a 37 km (23 miles) drive. I could not let Braxton go home without experiencing and seeing a kangaroo, Tasmanian devil, koala bears, emu, our poisonous snakes, and poisonous spiders. One thing I made him aware of, as it was our summer, is to always be on the lookout for snakes, and white tip tailed spiders inside or outside the home. To get bitten by either one could have deadly consequences. You should have seen the look on his face.

After our visit to the Sanctuary, we then toured around the Yarra Valley, which is a well-known Australian wine region, which attracts many tourists, and many weddings are held on these beautiful properties. On heading back we stopped at Lilydale cemetery to visit mum's graveside. I shared again, what a wonderful, loving person my Mum was as tears rolled down my cheeks.

I was excited for Braxton to attend church with me, and to introduce him to Dorothy, Dr. John Smith, Tan and Mark. One thing you have to realize about Australia is that there is not a huge percentage of people that attend church, yet the ones that do attend are not just the pew sitters every Sunday, but the ones that truly believe. In a post-Christian culture, there is no need to attend church so if you do it is because you are a believer. Christianity is not a religion, but a lifestyle. I was pleased that I was attending a church that spoke the truth. We attended the Sunday services and then went back again on Christmas Day which fell on a Monday. Australian churches hold services on Christmas morning.

Christmas Day was fast approaching and I was excited for Braxton to see how "Aussies" celebrate Christmas Day. After attending morning services on Christmas Eve Sunday, Christmas Day preparations were set into high gear. My sister, and sister-in-law, Julie (nicknamed "Harry"), had peeled bags of potatoes, pumpkins (butternut squash) and cooked our broccoli and cauliflower with cheese sauce, made a trifle, and steamed the plum pudding that dad made back in October. Plum Pudding needs to be made in advance for the flavors to permeate throughout. Plum pudding is not what most people think, as it consists of sultanas (golden raisins), mixed peel, spices, and currants. Plum Pudding originated in the 14th Century and is traditionally served at the end of a British Christmas dinner. As a kid, my mum would load our plum pudding with sixpences, and even though Australia changed over to decimal currency in 1966, mum would still place coins in our "pud" up until I was the age of 15. However, when our currency changed it was no longer "safe" to put coins in the plum pudding. How on earth, at such a young age we never swallowed a coin is beside me. The fun was to see who had collected the most money.

I love Christmas Day, not only for the meaning behind it, but to be with my family is the best thing ever. Our traditional meal is roast pork with crackling (rind), turkey, chicken, and a huge ham, roasted potato, pumpkin, beans, broccoli and cauliflower in cheese, and brown gravy. After our bellies were full, we headed outside in the sweltering heat for a game of cricket. Braxton was hilarious, as this was his first introduction to Aussie Rules Cricket. He got bowled not long after taking his turn to bat. He started to argue in good fun with the umpire, which happened to be my brother Rob. Needless to say, Braxton needs some more practice with cricket.

Our week was quickly coming to an end, and I tried to jam pack each day with fun and different things to see and do. We made a trip by train to downtown Melbourne as I wanted to show him my wonderful city and to also visit the places I had worked at. My positions varied, but I worked at the State Library of Victoria as well as for various solicitors (known as lawyers here). My travel to work was long and tedious. I would drive from Olinda (my hometown) to the train station at Ringwood which was a 35 minute commute, board a train which would take one hour, and walk about 10-15 minutes to my place of employment. This was only one way! I did this for ten plus years. I did notice that most people in rural Indiana live close to where their employment is, and traveling further than 20 minutes to work was not really the norm.

It was a gorgeous day in Melbourne, blue skies overhead, and the sun was shining. We stopped at an outside café, and ordered cappa's (Cappuccino's) as it was morning tea time. I proceeded to give Braxton a brief history of downtown Melbourne.

We meandered up to the State Library of Victoria, which opened in 1856, and was of neoclassical architecture. It truly is an amazing building, not to mention the grand reading room. I felt very privileged to of worked here for so many years, and to share this piece of history with Braxton.

Across from the state library was a new retail store called "Daimaru" which was owned by the Japanese and opened its doors in 1991. It was a huge shopping mall with very expensive items that no one could really afford. The upside to Daimaru is that this is where you could get the best sushi in Melbourne. Braxton did manage to pick up some Australian souvenirs from here to take back with him. I took him to visit the County Court, Family Court, and Supreme Court as I often frequented these places when working for solicitors. We got on one of Melbourne's iconic trams (like a cable car) and headed back down to Swanston Street, where I showed him where my mother had worked as an usher at the Capitol Theatre.

It was now getting close to lunchtime, and we went into one of the little cafes with the booth seating and the little jukeboxes attached to the wall. This is where Braxton experienced the famous Australian "Four 'N Twenty" meat pie and tomato sauce. Nicknamed "dogs eye, and dead sauce", and a plate of chips (steak fries). Australians use slang, and always abbreviate everything. After we finished lunch I saw that there was a Darrell Lea shop next door. Darrell Lea is an Australian company that manufactures chocolate and licorice, and is headquartered in New South Wales. It is a favorite of Australians, and the licorice is to die for. The company dates back to around 1917 and I am pleased to say that on the rare occasion I can find Darrell

Lea products in the States. Braxton loves lollies (candy) and especially the Cadbury, Mars, and Nestle chocolate that is sold only in Australia like "Cherry Ripe", "Crunchie", and "Violet Crumble".

It wouldn't be a visit downtown at Christmas time, unless we stopped and visited the Myer windows. It has been a Christmas tradition since 1956 to visit these windows that come to life. They have a different story every year. We got to see Roald Dahls *Charlie and the Chocolate Factory*, so cleverly done with such detail that you could feel as though you were right in the story. I still enjoy watching this movie.

At the last minute, I decided to take Braxton to the Rialto Tower. The Rialto reminds me of the Willis Tower in Chicago, where you can get amazing views over the skyscape buildings and surrounding areas. From here you could actually get a view of the TV towers on Mount Dandenong where I lived.

Chapter Ten

As we walked down Swanston Street heading back towards the train station, Braxton stopped out of the front of a jeweler by the name of Charles Rose. He looked at me and smiled, and said: "We are going in here". I said, "Yes!" After looking at so many different style rings, we choose an 18ct yellow gold handmade ring comprising of three round brilliant cut diamonds. It was exciting to be getting my engagement ring in Australia. I did need it re-sized, and we could either wait, or we could come back. Believe me, I was not coming back. I wanted that little rock on my finger. Ladies, I am sure you can relate when you get your engagement ring, you just cannot stop looking at it. I could not get back to my sisters quick enough to show everyone.

A few days later we took a drive out to Cockatoo to visit with my brother and his family, and to show off my ring. That evening we went out to eat, and Braxton ordered the Chicken parmigiana with chips and salad. The parmigiana was that huge it covered the entire plate. He still talks about this meal today, and he still has not had anything here that compares to it back home. Note: Braxton also got to try real fish and chips and a "hamburger with the lot".

My girlfriend Neats, and her husband Han's organized an Engagement Party for us at her home in Heathmont. I was surprised to see so many work colleagues, as well as all my family in attendance. Han's could really cook a mean barbie, and in true Australian fashion, we had the biggest prawns, homemade hamburgers, and sausages. A great selection of salads and desserts were passed around. Our gift was two beautiful pewter goblets with wattle and eucalyptus leaves on them. Braxton gave a speech and thanked everyone for their thoughtfulness, support, and love for me. His speech moved me to tears as he told everyone how beautiful I was, and how much I had meant to him.

Eight weeks before visiting Melbourne (October), Braxton began to search U.S. Immigration and Naturalization Service (INS) website Online to research the necessary steps and requirements for immigration. He was able to find out what forms and other documentation, the timetable, and the fees required for a citizen to sponsor a fiancé to America. Yes, he knew that I was the one, so the details of making two into one was his mission. Braxton studied the forms and instructions for completing them for over six months. He read, and re-read the step by step instructions and started to collect the necessary legal documents (both his and mine), and evidence required to complete the K-1 Visa application form. This form required birth certificates, passports, engagement ring evaluation, deposit receipts from our wedding photographer and reception place, an Affidavit of Support Form (I-134) also needed filling out with copies of Braxton's employment status, copies of bank statements.

The K-1 Visa allows a fiancé to immigrate to the States. Once in America, the couple is required to be married within 90 days. One other major requirement was required evidence that the couple had met each other in person previous to the application. So the pictures that were taken in July during my visit to Indiana and my airline ticket stubs became "Exhibit A", and Braxton's trip to Australia for Christmas 2000 which produced more photos and airline stubs became "Exhibit B" to satisfy this condition. All of this was being figured out before visiting me in Melbourne. Once he returned to Indiana, collecting together the documents and filling out very complex forms we would begin in earnest between February and April get on with the process. The very tricky part to all of this would be to try and set a wedding date and make the necessary arrangements to all take place within 90 days after my arrival which was a date only known by the INS. We set a July date, and hope that this would all magically fall within the government dictates and allowance. But that was not to be.

Braxton made arrangements to fly to Australia during his school holidays June to August 2001. I was not allowed to visit the U.S. until given the right to immigrate (another stipulation). To our surprise, the K-1 Visa application was approved just a week after it was filed in April, but there was another twist: I had to travel to the U.S. Consulate in Sydney (by appointment) and gain the State Department's official approval to travel to the U.S. This also required that I first submit an application form with documentation, and secondly to submit to a medical exam with a barrage of inoculation shots at a prescribed doctor in Melbourne's central business district, and then to wait for the date appointed to meet with the consulate. So during his visit to Melbourne, we had to prepare this form, get the medical, and collect the necessary documents. So what this meant is that any idea of a July wedding was off and we were once again having to reset the date, but this would have to be based upon the State Department's approval to leave. This would have to be decided later – the date only known by the U.S. officials.

The medical exam I had was not a pleasant experience, and I was glad Braxton had attended this with me. The doctor called me in, and he seemed to be very uneasy, and nervous. He had asked me inappropriate questions, and I stood my ground. At some stage in the exam room, he said, "Do you want your papers signed?" This was a threat. I said yes, but I wasn't agreeing with what he had suggested I do. I walked out, and he did sign my papers. I just could not believe what I just went through, and thought about younger women who were put in this situation, feeling threatened and naïve, and what they might have done to get their papers signed. I was furious and was going to take this further.

As it turned out my appointment with the U.S. Consulate came after Braxton had returned home. This experience was all left to me. I had to arrange travel to Sydney, accommodation, and have to survive the interrogation that awaited me that was not pleasant in the least. My appointment was 9:30 a.m. I had all my relevant documentation in hand. Besides a long distance relationship that proved to be a test on the heart, I was ready to face my next battle, and that was dealing with the U.S. Consulate. After getting through security on the ground floor, I proceeded to floor 27 for my appointment. A lady before me was already at the counter, and the waiting room was full of "alien's" as the U.S. liked to call us. I could see directly behind the immigration officer an in-tray labelled "reject", and one labelled "accept". The reject tray was spilling over, and the accepted one was practically empty. Enough to make anyone feel uneasy.

The immigration officer was loud, and yelling at a lady, and being very obnoxious. She was letting everyone know in the waiting room that she had the control. The lady turned to me, and said "I have been rejected", as she burst into tears. I replied, "I am so sorry". Then my turn came and I handed over my documents, she asked me if I knew the address of my husband's school where he was employed. I knew it was on U.S. 33 but did not have the exact number, to which she kept on asking, and I said that is all I know. She asked me why I wanted to marry this guy and move to the States, and I answered all her questions to the best of my knowledge. Now I had a question for her. I told her about the doctor who did my medical exam who was recommended by the U.S. Consulate, and that I would like to report him. She pretended not to hear me, so I repeated my question. Her reply eventually came and she said "Do you want to go and live in the States?" the famous line I heard from the doctor. I said I wanted him reported. She was quiet and did not say another word to me as she stamped my documents, and gave me the relevant documents for me to go live in the States. I did write a letter to both Consulates reporting this doctor, but I do not believe anything came of it.

As soon as I left the building I phoned Braxton to say that I had passed my interview, and was guarding my carry-on with all these important immigration documents. I caught a late flight back to Melbourne. After arriving at

Melbourne Airport, I got a shuttle to the overnight carpark (parking lot). As the shuttle was full, the driver recommended that all luggage must be placed in the trailer. No! My carry-on had my immigration documents, but he insisted so I complied. My car was located at carpark "C". We had stopped at "A", and "B" and I got off at "C" only to go to the back of the trailer to retrieve my carry-on, and to my utter disbelief, it wasn't there. By this time it was pouring down with rain, I said to the driver my carry-on is missing, and he asked, "Was it red? I replied, "Yes", and he said he saw it back at "B". He said you may want to run back and get it. Frantically I ran back, and it was quite a distance. The rain blinded my vision, and I prayed that my carry-on would be there. No guarantee of course, but low and behold there it was. I crouched down beside it and just sobbed. I was wet through, felt sick to my stomach, and slowly proceeded back to "C" carpark to locate my car.

As I somewhat composed myself, I headed out of the carpark and headed towards the City of Melbourne, or that's what I thought, only to find out I was heading towards Geelong in the opposite direction. With the rain pelting down on the windscreen (windshield) and with tears in my eyes, I could not see a thing. I remember pulling over and phoning my sister saying I was lost. She tried to calm me down and directed me as to which way I was to go. I arrived home very late, walked in, and sobbed about my day.

With all my documents in hand, I could now book a one-way ticket to the U.S. This time I was not booking with Japan Airlines. I decided to fly Qantas Airlines and had my ticket booked for September 11, 2001. I fully packed two suitcases, one carrying my wedding and bridesmaids dresses, the other stuffed full of my clothes. I had arranged earlier for shipment of my other goods and chattels, through a removalist (moving) company.

Chapter Eleven

I had received word that my flight to the U.S. had been cancelled and that air travel to the U.S. had been stopped. I quickly turned on the TV to see that a terrorist attack had taken place at the World Trade Center. It was terrible to watch, and I just stood there in a daze as both towers came tumbling down. I could not believe my eyes. My flight was rescheduled for September 27th.

Saying farewell to my family to take up my new life in another country was really tough. My nephews Bretto, Lukey, and my niece Mickie were all sobbing, as they stood on the verandah steps of their home watching me load my suitcases into the car. All of my family came out to the airport to farewell me on my departure. It was traumatic for all of us. They had all written me notes, but I told them I would read them on the plane. I did this from my flight from Melbourne to Los Angeles, and I sobbed like a baby. I was making a huge sacrifice with leaving family, friends, relatives, but deep down I knew all of this was a God thing. I had peace knowing that.

The U.S. Government had tightened up their security at airports after 9/11 and coming through customs on a one-way ticket through Los Angeles was stressful. I was put through the third degree, taken back into a little room (as Australians call it) where I sat for what seemed like hours, and interrogated once again. My concern was whether or not I would make my connecting flight to Chicago. I knew I had all the relevant required documents, and knew I was fine, but when dealing with these immigration officers, who like to have authority over you, I knew it would be in their timing as to when they would let me go. I observed other travelers sitting in this room from other countries, and noticed the majority of them were non-English speaking. These travelers were not treated well at all. Fortunately I was cleared and made my connection.

My arrival into Chicago was at a reasonable time. I then took the United Limo bus to South Bend Airport where Braxton would be picking me up. It had just been over two months since I had seen him.

We had been able to set a wedding date for November 3, 2001. I was thankful that Braxton and his mother had already booked the wedding venue, and had mailed out invites which I had helped pick out. I was excited that my brother would be walking me down the aisle.

My first couple of weeks living in the U.S. was quite the eye-opener. Braxton and I headed to Kendallville to order our wedding flowers, and after leaving the florist shop we quickly stopped at the supermarket and were checking out when I heard a siren go off. Everyone seemed to panic around me, so I asked him, "What is that siren?" He replied, "It's a tornado siren". He said, "We need to get out of here, and head back to Ligonier." As we drove back towards Ligonier, the weather seemed to be taking a turn for the worst, the skies were dark, the wind had picked up, and the rain had started to bucket down. We could no longer see out the front windscreen (windshield) or side windows so he pulled off onto the side of the road. The car was lifting off the ground, and it felt like the car was being hit by debris. What seemed to last like 15 minutes or so, it was probably only five minutes. I told him there and then that I wanted to go straight back to Australia. Braxton had prayed for our safety, and that no harm would come to us. Suddenly everything just stopped, the road was littered with branches off trees, limbs strewn across yards, and on houses. The road was blocked so we made a couple of detours, and eventually headed on our way again. We later found out that we had been in a Level 1 Tornado. The car came out without a scratch on it. Answer to prayer!

Chapter Twelve

Our wedding was held at Ligonier Evangelical Church by Rev. Hubert Harriman who performed the ceremony. This was the church that Braxton had attended for 22 years. We had counselling sessions beforehand with Rev. Harriman. One of the things he had us do was to write out five reasons as to why we want to marry this person, and five reasons as to why you want to marry this person now. He then wanted us to frame it. We have this in our bedroom, and it is a great reminder for both of us to revisit on a regular basis.

Like all weddings, there is something that never goes to plan. As my brother could not really be here for a fitting, his measurements were given over the phone to Braxton. The tuxes were to be delivered Friday evening during our rehearsal. We realized that they had forgotten my brother's jacket and his shoes. The firm guaranteed us that they would be delivered early Saturday morning.

Our wedding was 11:00 a.m. You guessed it! No jacket, and no shoes. My brother has huge feet and could not fit into anyone else's shoes. He had only brought a pair of runners with him. So he walked me down the aisle in his black socks, and no jacket. We laugh about this now, but at the time it had really stressed Braxton out. Me, not so much.

In Australia, our traditional wedding cake is fruitcake with fondant icing. I had our cake made by a lady that made cakes for the Waterford Crystal Company. She had also made a beautiful bouquet of handmade fondant flowers to adorn the top of it. I was happy to get a cake made in the U.S. but Braxton wanted me to have something from Australia. I had the cake made in May, as we were planning for a July wedding, only to find out that was not going to be the case. When Braxton visited in July, he actually took the wedding cake back with him on the plane. I was concerned the cake would not last until November. I was reassured by the baker that the cake itself would be fine. When it came time to cut the cake, it was rock hard. You could not even get a knife through it, because the fondant icing had become like a solid block of ice. Gladly most Americans do not care for fruitcake. Our tradition is to place a piece of fruitcake in a little cake bag and place it under your pillow that evening, and it will bring you good luck, and if you are single you would dream of your future spouse. Silly, I know!

We enjoyed a wonderful honeymoon in the Smoky Mountains, along with the bears. (That's another story!)

We were still dealing with Immigration issues, and I was due to have fingerprints taken again. This would be the tenth time having these done. I was also now applying for an Application for Employment which would allow me to work in the U.S. This would mean I would need to appear at the U.S. Department of Justice Office in Indianapolis for another interview. Failure to attend this interview would result in automatic termination of my application. It became a little joke between Braxton and myself, as every form that needed to be filled out, we would guess how much it would cost, and we were usually spot on. We filled out numerous applications that would incur a fee of $200 for each application. This was another depressing time seeing people who could not speak a word of English be treated like they had just committed a crime. This broke my heart. I went up to the window and as soon as Braxton spoke, and they realized he was American, I was treated like royalty. I hope and pray that all people going through this process are more respected today.

Now I had to file another application to remove the condition on my Residence (green) Card. The cost of the application fee was approximately $160; for the USCIS fee $500; and for biometrics $85. The fees continued to increase at each stage. The card had to be changed now as we were now married. This took approximately three months until I received my new green card, which by the way is really pink.

Braxton and I had been married for two years, and life was wonderful, exciting, and full of fun. We had plans to travel Europe during his school holidays. God obviously had other plans, in that I found out I was pregnant. I could not believe it. My chances of ever having children were very slim.

I was eight weeks along feeling great and was due for a routine checkup and ultrasound (because of my age) with the OB/GYN. I informed Braxton that he did not need to come with me and that everything would be fine. Low and behold, during my ultrasound the doctor looked concerned, and came back and told me that she had some sad news for me, and that our child did not have a heartbeat. I laid there in disbelief, and it felt as though time had just frozen. I gathered myself, put on the brave face, but my heart was truly broken. She recommended that I have a D & C and they scheduled that for the following week.

I remember getting to the car and just sobbing. I knew Braxton would phone me in his lunchtime to see how I got on, and so I was trying to compose myself before that time. I broke the news to him, and that evening the pastor and his wife came around, prayed, and read scripture to both of us. I remember the next few days just laying around on the couch, in a daze.

I remember hearing of women who have experienced miscarriages before, and just passed it off as "Oh they will have another child one day." I am so sympathetic to women that experience this. It is a hard lonely place to be in. I had no family here, was fairly new in this country, and felt downright miserable, and withdrew into myself.

But God! I got pregnant again, and it is important to note here that we had a one in twenty chance that we would have a Down syndrome child, and often got asked by the medical staff if we would want to have the test to find out. We had complete faith and trust in God and did not need any test.

I had morning sickness for five months, and the worst heartburn you could ever experience. I remember sitting at the funeral home when we were attending Braxton's aunt's funeral and here I was swigging Mylanta out of the bottle. People who were at this funeral still talk about it today.

,

Nine months could not come quickly enough. Because of my age I had numerous ultrasounds and was monitored very closely. Braxton would now come with me to all of my appointments. We prayed that God would bless us with a healthy child. I had a dream one night, that I had a son and he would weigh 8.5lbs, be born at 8:06 a.m., and he would be 19.5 inches in length. As soon as I awoke from this dream I scribbled this information down on a piece of paper, and the following morning showed Braxton.

On June 11, 2003, at 8:06 a.m. we were blessed with our miracle child Harrison Charles Savchuk, weighing in at 8.5lbs, length was 19.5 inches, and he was perfect. You cannot make this stuff up. But God!

What we thought were our plans, God had something else in store for us. While being older parents is sometimes difficult, we feel we are truly blessed by what God has given us. Harry has made our lives complete, and we love him unconditionally.

All you need is to have the faith of a mustard seed. In sharing this I want women to know that God is always there for you. I know many women dealing with infertility issues, miscarriages, and stillbirths. I did experience another miscarriage a year after having Harry. Never give up ladies. God has a wonderful plan for all of us. We just need to be still and listen to his quiet whisper.

Chapter Thirteen

Speed forward. Only good for fifteen years, my Green Card was coming up for renewal, and after much thought and consideration, I decided to apply to the U.S. Citizenship and Immigration Services (USCIS) to become a U.S. Citizen. Yet another form to fill out. I would still need to get biometrics, done once again, and supply all the relevant documents with the form. Fortunately, Australia is a country that allows dual citizenship.

I had my biometrics in Michigan City, and there I was handed a CD and booklet on the 100 Civic questions that I need to study. The officer informed me that I probably had about six months before I would hear from them. Not true! I received my letter outlining my interview time and date, in less than three months. I would also need to travel to Indianapolis for this interview.

I was not sure how this studying was going to go, as I have not done anything like this in years. Braxton and Harry spent countless evenings holding up random flashcards and asking me the questions. I remember celebrating the 4th of July on Lake Wawasee, in Syracuse with close friends, and each one of them would ask me random civic questions.

This day seemed to approach quickly, and I had myself decked out in my red, white, and blue outfit. I had many people from my church praying for me, but I was still a nervous wreck. I think not knowing what to expect was more my issue, than knowing the answers to the questions. Thankful that my sidekick Braxton was with me once again.

After getting through all the security, we proceeded to the 6th floor. One thing that seemed odd to me was that there was a long single line of people waiting to get into a lift (elevator). You do not just stand outside the lift doors, you had to take it in turns as to who was getting on. Security officers checked us both again, and we were directed where to sit and wait. Now the nerves were starting to rev up again, and within minutes my name was called. I knew Braxton was praying for me right there and then, and gave me one of his cute winks.

I met with the lovely (the treatment was really much kinder) immigration officer, and she tried to make me feel at ease. She spoke about the weather, and how she was from California. Enough of the small talk I thought. I need to get this thing over and done with. The first part of the test consisted of three components: speaking, reading, and writing. I now understood what the small talk was all about, she was observing my ability to speak English. Phew! I knew I had passed that one. I then had to read three sentences correctly to show that I had the ability to read in English, and thirdly for the writing part I had to write out three sentences to show my ability to write in English. I was hoping that the Civics part of the test was written, as I am a visual learner, but found out that she was to ask the questions verbally. I knew to pass I would have to get six questions correct. I answered all six questions correctly. I had passed the test. The whole procedure only took about half hour. Braxton looked surprised when I walked out, as I had not been gone long. I gave him the thumbs up, and smiled from ear to ear. Next step I would receive a letter in the mail, with the date and time of my Naturalization Oath Ceremony which would be held at the U.S District Courthouse in Fort Wayne. She indicated that this should take place sometime the next month.

After waiting for less than a month I received my letter stating that my Naturalization Ceremony would be held September 11, 2015. How ironic this seemed when I mentioned earlier that this was the date I was to arrive in the States, and that was cancelled, and now here I am attending my Naturalization Ceremony on that date. God had it all worked out. I was so excited and glad I had my husband and son with me. This was a very emotional day for me as my name was called, and I went forward before the U.S. District Court Judge, and took the oath in front of everyone in the room. I was then presented with my naturalization certificate.

After the ceremony, I had to proceed to the Social Security people who had a table set up outside the courtroom doors to get my condition removed from my social security card, as now I was a U.S. Citizen. In my package, I had also received the relevant information as to what was required to obtain my U.S. Passport.

From immigration to citizenship was a very stressful time, not only for the applicant, but to the family filling out all the application forms and official appointments. We were always at their beck and call. If you failed to fill out the forms correctly or failed to attend an interview, or an appointment, it could be mean a big delay. You had to drop everything.

With all the applications, airfares, doctor visits, and biometrics it cost us approximately $15,000 (conservatively). But in the end, God made the way straight and each step of the process was timely approved and it made for a great story. Looking back now one can laugh, but the process of legally immigrating to the U.S. is complicated, time consuming, and costly.

Chapter Fourteen

I believe without a doubt that God allowed for our paths to cross just at the right moment, and for me to be saved. I am content, and grateful to God for giving me the privilege of loving someone who loves me in return. Our love is deep and beyond meager words to describe. We have similar interests, so getting along with each other and loving each other is easy. We are truly soulmates. Both our prayers had been answered beyond our wildest expectations. I love my boys, and I am truly not deserving of such a gift. But God!

I am blessed to be involved in a wonderful church – Grace Community. This Church has been instrumental in deepening my faith and nurturing my walk with God. It would be remiss of me not to mention my prayer warriors, Annie, Shali, Melissa, Mama Shari, Tammy, Natalie, Dana, Catherine, and Shelbi.

Also our neighbors Karen and Gerald who are always helping us out whether it is babysitting the dog, mowing our lawns when we are on vacation, or watching over our home when we travel back and forth to Australia.

If you are reading this book, and do not have a relationship with God I encourage you to find a church that preaches the truth.   Ask lots of questions, and dig deep into the inerrant word of God's book – The Bible.

You! Yes You! Are loved and cherished by God no matter what your past looks like. God will never leave you or forsake you.

"Be strong and courageous. Do not be afraid or terrified because of them, for the LORD your God goes with you; he will never leave you nor forsake you." (Deuteronomy 31:6)

This is a poem Braxton had written to me on my arrival to the United States on 2 July 2000.

Shelley,

"You are the summer sun rising in the Eastern sky;

Resplendent and radiant are the rays of your earthly form

You are the fullness of the midnight moon at fall's great harvest,

That mandates the ebb and flow of thoughts made profound by love.

You are the stars on a clear crisp winter night.

The brilliant luster of which illuminates the limitless bounds of your never dying soul.

Sun, moon, and stars;
Body, mind, and soul...

You are the universe in microcosm,

And in you, I embark on a Voyage of true love –
A journey determined by divine destiny;
A journey of ultimate discovery.

Sun, moon, and stars;
Body, mind, and soul...
In, by, and through you I discover myself and all that is good.
I love you."

ABOUT THE AUTHOR

Shelley Savchuk was born and raised in Melbourne, Australia. Shelley now resides in the United States.

After graduating from Cames Business College she was employed 38 years as a secretary at a solicitor's (lawyer's) office, the State Library of Victoria, Catholic College, Sale, and in the Catholic Education Office before immigrating to America.

Shelley is a keen motor racing enthusiast and driver, and you would be sure to find her every year at the Australian Formula One Grand Prix. Shelley belonged to the Victorian MG Car Club and participated in many car racing events in her MGBGT. Shelley loves to volunteer at her church in women's ministry, her son's school, and provide meals for people less fortunate than herself. Shelley is such an encourager to many who meet her and is always doing a random act of kindness for someone.

Shelley keeps young with one son who is 15.

Shelley has a great sense of humor, is adventurous, and fun to be around.

EPILOGUE

After seven months of failing health, I received word the first week of May that my dad was to be admitted in a palliative care center. The physicians could do no more. I made arrangements to fly to Melbourne once again and set out on the morning of May 15. While in transit to O'Hare International Airport I received a text from my sister that my dad had died just after midnight there (May 16) just after 10am here.

The saddest trip I have ever travelled, I was re-united with family and assisted with the funeral arrangements. So with the writing of this memoir a significant chapter of my life is closed.

But God continues to direct my path as my story continues.

Made in the USA
Lexington, KY
23 July 2018